HOW TO CURE INSOMNIA

Professor Sheridan Simove MD, BAA, NAP

1

2

3

4

5

6

7

8

9

10

11

12

13

14

15

16

17

18

19

20

21

22

23

24

25

26

27

28

29

30

31

32

33

34

35

36

37

38

39

40

41

42

43

44

45

46

47

48

49

50

51

52

53

54

55

56

57

58

59

60

61

62

63

64

65

66

67

68

69

70

71

72

73

74

75

76

77

78

79

80

81

82

83

84

85

86

87

88

89

90

91

92

93

94

95

96

97

98

99

100

Lightning Source UK Ltd.
Milton Keynes UK
UKOW02f2140290316

271117UK00001B/1/P

9 781845 496821